For

I s

That
Bad?

reflections
of a
grumpy
optimist

stuart hulse

with doodles by the author

hope "wedding in Reading im print was good!

imprint illyria books

Stuart Hulse

September 2016

www.imprintillyria.com

Published by imprint illyria books

First published 2011

Printed and bound by CPI Antony Rowe,
Eastbourne

ISBN 978-0-9558247-6-0

im/rint illyria books
London

Dedication

For Oliver
my eldest grandson
and an avid reader.

Appreciations

With thanks to Laurence Bradbury,
Sue Luker, Elaine Fairless, Alexandra Hulse,
Simon Ashley and Laurence Phillips.

Contents

Foreword

by Peter Hughes

Stuart Hulse has really written his own foreward in the opening lines of his poem, *Poet*: "I am the poet/Of my own persona."

The satisfaction of this anthology is that these are the poems of all our personas. In exposing so much of his life, Stuart makes so much of ours only too recognisable. It's just that few of us have the honesty to bare as much of ourselves as Stuart does, let alone possess his succinctness in doing so.

Here are reflections on the eternal themes – love, marriage, infidelity, loneliness, bereavement – but here too is the melancholy of ageing with both the wisdom (*Conversation*) and nostalgia (*The Shops*) that attend it.

Here is the mid-life crisis (*Is it that bad?*), the joy of fatherhood (*Son*), and odes to a sports car (*XJS*) and football (*Arsenal*).

These are poems for anyone who has loved, grieved or been in debt, the dentist's chair or to Highbury. In short they are the poems of Everyman.

Occasional poet, Peter Hughes is an award-winning writer, broadcaster & founding editor of ITV's iconic 'Wish You Were Here?' A regular contributor to The Times and Daily Telegraph and leading magazines, he lives in central London by the River Thames.

Is it that bad?

I receive up to five complex solicitors'
letters on average a week
I have bought a house
I can't really afford
It is in a William IV square
in Kennington
My business is losing about fifty per cent
of its income

I left my wife fifteen months ago
My teenage children now distrust my
love for them
I have just been suddenly let down
on a major corporate deal
This has cost me £125,000
in the short term
I do not have a secretary (they leave)
I have been recruiting for two vital job
appointments simultaneously

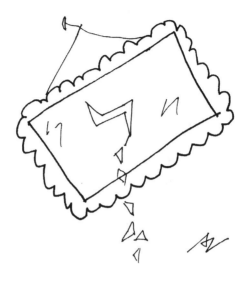

My day-to-day RHP at the office
is pregnant
I have a bridging loan of £50,000
for a house purchase

I pick my spots
I bite my lip
My ex-wife has yet to agree on financial
arrangements

I have just commenced a mortgage with
repayments of £1,875 per month
I see a (now casual) psychotherapist
My personal effects are located in four
places.

I partly live with a lady I employ
I smoke too much
I drink too much
I am having expensive and extensive
building work done on the new house
This requires up to six decisions a day
I have just secured a new £125,000 bank
overdraft on my business

My family are currently leaving the sold
family home in Surrey
I bought an engagement ring which has
been rejected and is in a drawer
My lady friend plans to rent her house
and live with me

I am actively seeking new business
My company's cash flow could nosedive
by July

My daughter is taking her A levels
I am due to captain the 'old' village
cricket team this season
I cannot afford to furnish my new home
My car radio has been stolen
My watch face is cracked

I am overweight
My breath gets short
I had (or have been told I had) three
nervous breakdowns in two years

I was divorced three months ago
I have given my TV to my son
My girlfriend is an independently
minded aristocrat and keeps it a semi-
secret
(We married in 1987 and remain so...)
I just ruined my aunt's cherished picture
I dislike my third-rate office
accommodation in Fleet Street

I am looking for better but inexpensive
new offices
I have just bought two stuffed
kingfishers

I am in love
I am confident
I am positive
I am too self-centred
I eat too much red meat

I Will Survive?

On a day in 1986

Conversation

Never say a word too much
Or leave unsaid what's true,
Listen as the problems flow
And say to yourself "what's new?"

Answer when the time is ripe,
Inject a joke or two,
Reason only when it's just
And count the insults few.

Feather someone else's nest,
Smile the stories through,
Contemplate what has been said
Let reflection turn the screw ...

The Shops

It is a grey November morning in
Rosendale Road,
The ghosts of VE Day street parties still
resting
As up the street I hurry along the wide
pavement
Past the regular tree trunks, to the shops.

The reassuring row of wooden-framed
windows;
Grocer, chemist, tobacconist, butcher,
ironmonger,
All family-named after a brown-coated
proprietor,
With forecourts swept clean beside the
solitary post box.

Floating along a slight wind reels a
cigarette card,
Lost from a boy's collection of sporting
heroes,
Overtaking a cracked marble lying in the
gutter
And unnoticed by the coalman's horses
cluttering past.

There are few shoppers to spot my
discovered treasures,
As happy as a sweets coupon from the
ration book,
Or the luxurious lilt of Vera Lynn's
plaintive songs
Echoing past the fresh vegetable display
at Lucking's.

Mr Pretlove, Mr Mason, Mr Brown;
shopkeepers and friends,
Whose sons and daughters went to fight
the war;
Who had feared the silent moment in a
doodlebug's flight;
All gathered in a steadfast line, up the
road.

Two Bridges, Dartmoor, 1994

Cricketers

Players please the Gentlemen
Cricketers please themselves
Bowlers are the archers
Batsmen the bastions
Keepers hold the field
Fieldsmen swim the outgrass
And the umpire is always correct.
Now you can even make a bet.

1982

Omnipotent Obolensky

'Soviet' and singular?
Brass plaques placed triangular:
Heritage - Rugby legend –
Wartime flyer.
The oval ball held regular;
A sculptor so particular…

A wingman's strong torso,
Hurricane's wing rising more so,
A pilot's death blow
When landing all those years ago.

Two top-ten tries,
Giving the All Blacks
A Twickenham surprise;
Now no-one denies his short-lived genius.

Blond dashing heart-throb Russian,
Yet English, all of a sudden;
A Prince of pace, truly iconic,
Before that tragic demise.

His light blue eyes closed forever…
But a memorial any one can see.

Greaves

Jimmy Greaves is on the Box
Probably wearing his football socks.
Ian St. John is talking easy
Solving problems that make Clough
queasy.

He was the striker most supreme
Darting like fish in a stream.
I saw him in his early days
When the great Jack Kelsey he amazed.

... My grandmother loved him

Muse

Musicles rolls on the kitchen floor,
Prostrate beside a scratched old door.
Rubbing the shoes,
Sniffing for news;
Her white front searching for strokings
more.

Musie's resigned as an average cat,
Preferring to travel as basically fat.
Licking the tap,
Rushing the flap;
Her custom is scoring the bathroom mat.

Muse is a teapot bereft of a bag,
Closely escaping the role of a hag.
Caressing the knee,
Requesting a fee;
Her stance resists the ordinary tag.

Muse is a friend of steadfast wish;
She prefers the pellets to any old fish.
Seeking the fire,
Rejecting the dire;
Her knowledge equates to a gourmet's
dish.

Musicles fears the black and white,
From whom she flees with all her might.
Scoffing the feed,
Relishing the need,
Her poise avoids a common fight.

Musie says bye from up on the stairs
And rises to bed to dream of affairs.
Patrolling the shrubs,
Ignoring the snubs;
Her interest confirmed by those curious
stares.

Muse is happy within her place,
Disporting a beauty about the face.
Dipping the paw,
Sleeping some more;
How does she ever stand the pace!

Without Father

Father seen on distant prairie
Out of focus, out of mind
Still the bitter taste so vacant
Empty space alone to find.

When into nothing divides a lifetime
Lonely half in brain and body
Just a sketchy described person
Thought of badly, told as shoddy.

Lament the missing days of honour
Endure a space left empty ever
And wonder in the heart to know
If he is brave and kind and clever.

I have never met my father
1994

Daisy - in Memoriam

About my mother who died in 1968
Remembered on Good Friday, 1997

Whenever there are pauses,
A dip in time's tick-tock,
I remember her devotion;
Her pose in forties frock.

To gather in the moments,
Not easy to recall,
Some underfelt, some crispy clear;
The kitchen and the downstairs hall.

Whatever made the funeral
So stark and fixed in time,
Results from endless bravery;
A woman's loyalty sublime.

To fester at the illness,
The doctors and the knife,
Cherishes her bitter pill;
Her laughter in a life of strife.

The memory of her strengthens,
Three decades known and lost;
Forever true and perfect known,
Determined not to count the cost.

Run Peacock Run

When you're chasing peacocks,
Or even white hens,
You have to run fast,
At the high speed of Ben's -
Record.

A llama or two;
Lazy fat pigs, it's true!
And a five-week-old bunny
For lots of strokes, yet no money
To pay.

Head over heels, and reels
On the jumping trampoline...
Such a glorious scene,
Then Ben on the slide,
Grandi beside, looking.

For Ben, after a visit to Finkley Down Farm
August 2011

$$\frac{5}{7} \times \frac{14}{15} + \frac{1}{3} =$$

Son

Tie the knot Tom
Ten minutes to go,
Schoolboys mustn't
Be slow.

Kick the ball Tom
Three goals to show
That daddies are human
And slow.

Turn the page Tom
Six sums to flow
And multiply the fractions
You don't know.

Pull up your trousers Tom
So much you grow,
And smile for your Mummy
Who loves you so.

1980

Lunchtime

Well, melody;
it plays some lunchtime tunes
While others take
sandwiches
To their desks.

Well, thought;
it primes instead of fumes
When young ones fret
about the time
In insecure communes.

June 1997

Drunk

Drink the bottle
Drain the can

Dip the pocket
Don the cap

Drive the auto
Drag the gear-stick

Droop the stomach
Drop the flab

Drone the barmaid
Dare the joke

Dangle the fiver
Dingle the poke

Damn the brain cells
Deliver the yoke
Farewell. Old chap.

1980

Spin Doctor

How many ways there are to be
So numerous are the sights to see
How constant are the changes made
So frequent in the butterfly plaid.

The smile, the concern,
the wriggling worm
And inside deeply true and firm
The flexibility to conform
And ego balanced out of norm.

Reflecting others day by day
To give them
a smile to play
While in one self
there is the need
To satisfy a selfish creed.

1986

Song of Blue

There is a spirit
False and true
Inside the motion
Green and blue

There is a time
Lonely and true
Under the apples
Pink and new.

There is a forest
Black and blue
Across the hills
Green and few.

There was a man
Khaki and glue
Around the world
Pale and untrue.

There is a person
Scarlet and true
Inside the life
Bright and blue.

Blue is my favourite colour

Early Summer

When May to
June
Comes into focus
Clearly
The leaves have
Sprouted
And the oak
is pouted
Grass is undercut
And the dew
so happy
It has many
a resting
To keep it
Skidaddie.

In hospital, May 1984

Boredom

Yawning through the morning
Sitting all day long
Snatch a breath of sunshine air
Compose another whistled song.

Reading newsprint headlines
Some articles as well
Glance into a speaking room
Wait for the telephone bell.

Walking into the artroom
Hopeful of some action
Glance from lady of OT
Brings boredom as reaction.

In hospital

PR Girl

The PR Girl,
Her lipstick perfect
and the bum rounded,
Challenging for a line.

Will she marry a star,
Her picture in the paper?
And the dress discussed –
Such coverage divine.

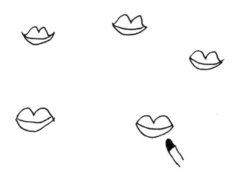

1997

Weekend

Frankly look upon the lawn
And say that this is home;
By next weekend the weeds will grow,
An answer to another flow.
That gifts a different form,
To City combinations
Left behind ...

Explosion

Beyond the summit of the mind,
Outside the prison of technology,
The equal pattern
Of mankind,
Is waiting.

Inside the walls of London town,
The forlorn and the feral find,
The freedom unknown
Of their kind,
Still waiting.

Ere long the hatred of the blind,
Trapped in a mental constipation,
The tension planted
Unrefined,
And waiting.

Beyond the peak of frustration,
Carved in a stone of manipulation,
The morning invisible,
Unawoken
And baiting.

1986

Reagan

El Presidente
Compton of the cream
Brilliant front man
For the galactic machine.

1984

Arsenal

The ecstasy of the moment,
The gunners in their red;
The Logie darting like a fish,
The Eastham of the lake.

Oh, Brady you departed
A staple cutting through,
But back to you my Charlie
The brilliant and the true.

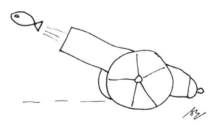

1982

Boris in Winter

Up on the white hills,
The blanket mist
Backdropping
The icy petrified branches;
We parked Boris.

He was new and
Four times four,
Made for the conditions;
Bottle green in
An arctic landscape.

We left him in
The frozen picnic park,
Bereft of popcorn, people
And Diet Coke;
Statuesque in the deserted fields of ice.

The walk was testing
And the ears hurting,
As we contemplated
Those rounded windy rises
Before turning back.

Exmoor in January
Uninviting;
Yet the Jeep leapt into life
And cruised away
To the warming pub.

Alex was disappointed ...

Exmoor, January 1996

XJS

Where's my white lady
Superficial in her beauty,
Powerful and pristine.

Where is my ton girl
Virgin and twelve-stroked,
Lusting speeder supreme.

Where's my blanche
Jaunty and thrusting;
Surely fulfilling a dream.

Where is my manhood,
Stereo-ed toughness;
Now that I've sold my queen?

Having sold the car in 1980

Infidelity

The fingers lie
Between the breasts
The nipples pouted through.

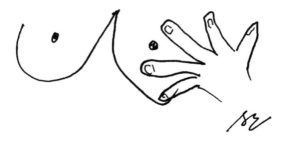

Jesus Christ,
Is that the time?
I've got to be home by two.

July 1997
in reflection

Fare Well

We will make our fond goodbyes
Again
Until the next hellos,
Squeeze the hand
and lip the cheek,
Find words so difficult
to speak,
yet sure that
love still grows.

1997

Universal Love Cage

I inhabit the love cage,
A brutalised budgerigar?
Shaking the bars
Swinging on the perch
Love this way
Or that - lurching lurching
Captured
By desire
A capsule on fire,
The moon around a planet
Enclosed in its rotation
Spun from an everyday universe
Against those iron bars,
Held by the stars
Of infatuation;
A pain-pricked prisoner;
Locked up, deep rooted, saluted?
Ever requited by
Love lashes that made the scars.

Candidate

Am I your compromise
candidate?
The essence
of a chosen
mate?

Or will you
admit
There was love
In the shit
that you
threw,
And will
the dark
earth rise
up again
Towards the
covering
blue?

Because you
can't stop
me loving
you
And I can't
force you
to be
true.

1986

Alex into Midnight

Alex into midnight
Two days in a row
The edge of sustainment
Beyond the void.

Alex into midnight
Two forces of sharpness
The brink of enjoyment
About the egos.

Alex into midnight
Two factors adjoining
The limit of loyalty
Unto the moment.

Alex into midnight
Two stories of agility
The claw of feline
Upon the beauty.

Alex into midnight
Two lives considered
The soul of decision
Around the charisma.

Alex into midnight
Two essays in reason
The bounds of boyhood
Along the discourse.

Alex into midnight
One choice insistent
The song of excitement
Under the happiness.

On a train to Norwich,
January 1985

Soccer Souls

Are you the Ferguson
Of my frustration,
And myself the waiting
Wenger?

Bring me my clean sheet,
Start
Bring the chants of the bored;
Put relegation

Firmly to the sword ...

Ring of Wild Water

The engagement ring
was placed in the top
drawer
of the dressing table
unworn,
Nestled by limp
bras
and unwashed socks.

It had been
put on ice.

The excited selection
of the angular art deco
cuts;
The crouched proposal,
lost
in rejection and examination,
put on probation.

I thought of it,
there
when I looked at
her naked finger.

Tabary's Tale

Sète-side under the
Unsettled sun,
Table primulas prettyful
By the cars' parking run.

Rain clouds low-heavy to
Dampen the pavements;
Their cafe-fun interrupted -
Cette's sensations, suddenly undone.

Come, buy, casual promenaders;
Sit here by table-tops, plum.
Just vin rouge du maison?
Go on, simply succumb...to

Languedoc the lazy, where
Every oyster is a moule's chum,
Heavenly cheese-grilled, together
And beckoning, beckoning – do
Come!

Mouth Man

Looking in those people's
mouths,
An endless search
for wrong;
Has made a dentist's
daily round,
Ten guineas for a song.

Pumping up the busy
drill,
So questing for
a probe;
Would make the toothless
beggar wish
That he could buy the globe.

After many years in the chair, 1997

Towards a Better Day

I said to you Andrew
In our open way.
As conversation
Began another day.

That I was tired Andrew
And devoid of play.
As consternation
Started yet another day.

I looked to you Andrew
In our studied way.
As reflection
Pierced the clouds away.

I turned to you Andrew
As you eased the way.
For painful
Things to say.

You brought the tears Andrew
On the mornings of grey.
So moving
Towards the better day.

I think of you Andrew
In my mind's play
As realisation
Turns the field to hay.

About conversations
with Dr. Andrew Powell, 1985

Patterns

(a message to myself)

Whenever things go wrong,
Remember from the past
That patterns never set so right
And you were sometimes last;
So give the life a lasting touch
Lifted by your heart;
It's not so bad as you may think,
So still play that target part.

Poet

I am the poet
Of my own persona,
The puppet
Of my own personality.

I am the tree
Of my own earth,
The trunk
Of my own perpetuality.

I am the man
Of my own mother,
The child
Of my own destiny.

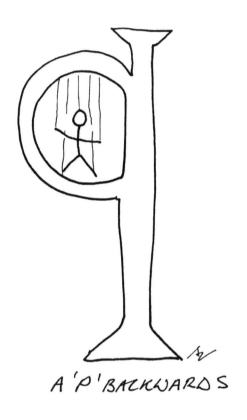

A 'P' BACKWARDS

I am the mandarin
Of my own empire,
The serf
Of my own mentality.

I am the prisoner
Of my own village,
The warden
Of my own concentration camp.

1986

Instant Request

A poem is sought
By The Torygraph
For the front page of
'ART', coming up this week.

Well, anything for a laugh...

"Fax it over in two hours,"
is demanded - blimey!
Sweat, then it's the coldest of showers!

Where to compose such instant verse
About what's happening around the
globe?
Or even rehearse, with a pal?

Yes, just over the road –
The Poetry Cafe; a place
For a fair-priced wine
And musings sublime...

But I'm more a hack than a 'Motion',
Though a pupil of Laureate Duffy.
So, scan the world in a hurry,
Scribble with a pre-internet flurry.

Rapidly get it over, at 1430.
Not a bestest piece;
Never tardy, however, and well to time.

On Saturday; with the newspaper:
A casual perusal, not of news
Or political views;
Yet the search for my rushed lines
In print, is fallow.
Perhaps they might have been too
shallow?

Only mild curses follow

Long Time Gone

When I was young
The months were long
And terms eternity.
The snow was deep, the summer hot;
A rabbit leapt into the pot,
And Christmas was a revelry.

Then I advanced
To middle age
And weeks flew ever by.
The rain is thin, the sunshine burns;
Trains seem to miss their turns,
And Santa's told some lies.

Missing Phil

I heard the Birds sing
Through the chapel windows
At Phil's celebration;
Togetherness at the sunshine,
Seaside gathering.

Sincere sparrows, indeed,
Joining his friends
To honour a light touch
Of integrity
And most modest knowledge.

Phil's donation of such generous spirit
Had merited that tribute -
Ray-beamed to the heavens.

...and even when his friends die,
There will be shared memories;
Passed on,
So always someone
Will rejoice in his excellence.

Soldier

I see the lonely soldier
Trudging up the stairs,
Six thousand miles to reach HQ,
More ironing than affairs.

We note the half-baked bachelor
Buying meals for one,
Eight hours to link upon the phone,
And barmaids aren't much fun!

November 1997

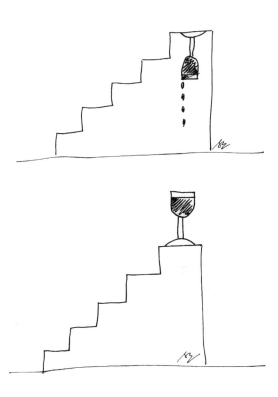

73

A Fair Affair

(1)

Strangers compare
her affair
with Rombaire
with the love of Burton for Taylor.

As she strives for
success -
No dressage distress,
Daring to challenge failure.

Ron's a mild-mannered
chap,
unlikely to flap,
showing beauty of form
for his trainer.

Now approaching his peak,
some observers will speak
that his rider must be a believer;
that red rosettes await
on the grand prix date –
His fate:
to be Alex's saviour.

Dear Ronnie, so sweet,
Such manners and style;
Be true, through and through
..... to her smile.

Forever The Fair Rombaire

(2)

When Ronnie comes galloping by,
Full shod, so fit, in fantasy,
Soon since Good Friday's date to die;
The lift of his head, mane dancing,
Handsomely groomed as said,
Ears dressage-perked through the
cloudy-grey sky...

And as much as I try
With a tear in each eye
It's impossible to resist
His golden beckoning.
Leap over his saddle-less rump –
Just jump!
The full eighteen hands.
"Hold fast my thighs!"
With never a looking back.

by Alex

Our unicorn friends on high
See down, where the river bends below
And whisper:
"Here come the princely Rombaire and
Alex,
Inseparable spirits,
Magically reunited,
Full-mannered, glide-riding by..."

Easter Day is not a lie!

Horse

Ever tried to draw a horse?
Of course.

Enough of these lies,
The equine denies
An artist like me.

Suitable to saddle,
Uncomfortable to ride;
Stupidly full of pride.

Fetlocks are part
of this voluminous art.
Ever heard a horse fart?

It rhymes.

Which is more than a horse does.

1980

Unmellow
Yellow

My favourite colour is now
Yellow,
Bigger than blue,
The one I loved.

The clear day's ocean –
sky blue,
Blue moons,
Reflected in dark blue
Lagoons...

Much liked, but
Overtaken
By the blue window's
Round, round, complete
Yellow sun.

Yellow, so distinct in
an azure background,
Leaping out of any tree's
Autumn brown.

Yellow penetrates, so
Light and confident, fresh,
Its upright sunflower
In praise of a
Yellowfull, sunglasses' sun:
Sometimes piercing pale, pale
...blue eyes.

Christmas Cheer?

Will you make it plain
Dear Sir
That Christmas is
The time of year
When restaurants and
Bars galore
From inland to the farthest shore
Give modest food
And dodgy wine
Make packets in a sting sublime
For all our Xmas cheer?

Author's Notes

on the Poems

Conversation *Page 13*

A charming friend Audrey Horne, who is 80 plus, says she reads this before attending a cocktail party.

The Shops *Page 14*

This was written under the guidance of Carol Ann Duffy (before she was appointed Poet Laureate) while staying at a hotel on Dartmoor, Devon; it recalls the atmosphere of Rosendale Road, Dulwich, South London towards the end of the Second World War.

Cricketers *Page 17*

Up to the 1960s, county cricketers were either Players (professionals) or Gentlemen (amateurs, usually from Oxbridge). There was an annual match at Lord's between them. England captains were always Gentleman until Len Hutton became the first Professional appointed, in the early 1950s. In earlier times betting on the game was illegal.

Omnipotent Obolensky *Page 19*

A memorial statue of rugby legend and pilot Prince Alexander Obolensky was unveiled in Ipswich, Suffolk, by my wife, his niece, Alexandra in 2009. Brendan Gallagher of the

Telegraph described sculptor Harry Gray's style as ironically 'soviet', since Obolensky had been a Russian-born aristocrat! The torso support echoes an RAF Hurricane fighter's wing, evoking the 24-year-old's fatal war-time crash landing near Ipswich in 1940. The *Daily Telegraph* ranks Obolensky's two 1936 tries against New Zealand in their all-time top 10; *The Times* called him a genius.

Greaves *Page 18*

The great goal-scorer – whom my Victorian grandmother Jane Glover loved, enjoyed a TV pundits' duo with Ian St. John.

Muse *Page 20*

Valentine's Day celebration of a tabby called Muse; her sister Zing (from "amusing") ran away or was abducted in Battersea, London.

Without Father *Page 22*

I never met my father; I was told he died in the early 1980s.

Daisy – in Memoriam *Page 23*

About my brave mother who died aged 53 having been savagely operated on for tuberculosis in her thirties, before curing drugs were created. My grand daughter Sasha Daisy carries on the lovely name; my mother's elder sisters were Lilly and Ivy; the three names were popular in Edwardian days. Both lived in to their nineties.

Run Peacock Run *Page 25*
For my second grandson Ben, when five, after a successful visit to Finkley Down Farm, Andover.

Drunk *Page 29*
Working closely with "the media", I had long witnessed alcohol worshipped in Fleet Street and at many late-night venues.

Spin Doctor *Page 30*
Decades in PR and the media can result in scepticism...even regrets?

Song of Blue *Page 32*
Blue was my favourite colour; however, read Mellow Yellow on page 80 to see how this may have changed recently!

Early Summer *Page 35*
A seasonal optimistic feeling in hospital in May 1984.

Boredom *Page 36*
A spell in hospital may be tedious.

Explosion *Page 40*
Though written in 1986, this could today be about the expanding 'underclass'.

Reagan *Page 42*
A certain similarity, perhaps: my boyhood sporting hero and the ultimate PR puppet.

Arsenal *Page 43*
Refers to Charlie George of the long hair and other players gone by. Irishman Frank Stapleton was The Gunners' swift striker.

XJS *Page 46*
Penned after having to sell the supercar (capable of 0 to 60 mph in 5.9 seconds) in 1980 for financial and business reasons.

Infidelity *Page 48*
In rueful and forlorn reflection of frequent unfaithfulness during my first marriage.

Fare Well *Page 49*
When I had agreed to my wife going to work in Hong Kong for Reuters for a year - we visited each other every two months.

Ray, partly for his god daughter (and writer) Liz Bird, whom I took on her first press trip, and for aviation writer Ray Hankin, former colleague of Phil's and latter-day PR man. I once shared a flight deck with him when Freddie Laker's Carvair car ferry aircraft was put into a deliberate stall over Stansted during a test flight and fell through the clouds like a brick.

Soldier *Page 72*
Feeling sorry for myself while my wife was living 7,000 miles away.

A Fair Affair (1) *Page 74*
Forever the Fair Rombaire (2) *Page 76*
'Rombaire' (stable name 'Ronnie') was Alexandra's much-loved dressage competition horse, which had to be destroyed, aged just 11, in 2009. She missed him terribly. (When a teenager, Alex had enjoyed times with Elizabeth Taylor and Richard Burton on their yacht.)

Horse *Page 78*
Both my wives have loved and owned horses and both suffered nasty accidents when riding.

About the Author

Born in South London during Britain's Finest Hour, Stuart Hulse has earned his living in the media world for several decades. Winning a scholarship to Dulwich College, he became a madrigal chorister and Festival Hall soloist, a sports colour, CCF platoon commander and prized artist, but was *'too lazy to study Latin hard'*! He was also a student at St. Martin's School of Art, London.

From a journalistic debut on City daily *Lloyd's List*, Stuart lived parallel lives as writer and broadcaster and founder of a PR and marketing agency for some of the biggest names in travel.

A first book of verse *Poems in Mid Life* was published in 1998. Post Fleet Street, Stuart and his wife Alexandra Obolensky, a former colleague and equestrienne of White Russian heritage, ran a fashionable gift boutique in Farnham, Surrey. They now live in the small Georgian town of Odiham, North Hampshire.

He has a son and daughter by his late ex-wife Malvene and has three grandchildren. Pleasures include soft cycling, Philharmonia Orchestra concerts, politics, wine, cricket and Arsenal and visiting the Languedoc. He is irritated by Americanisms or miss-pronunciation of English and by any lack of good manners. 'Grumpy'? - almost certainly...

THE GRANARY, MONK'S YARD, ODIHAM, HAMPSHIRE, RG29 1LY

TEL: 01256 703705 EMAIL: STUALEXHULSE@HOTMAIL.COM

MOBILES: AH - 07753 808536 SH - 07887 700772

2.9.16

'the real deal' —
you're so literary ...!
Tell your contacts it's
on Amazon books - poetry ...

Steve

Last Word

A multiple personality.

E. Grange   *Form Master.*

The form master at Dulwich College who scribbled this insightful remark at the foot of Stuart Hulse's school report in 1956 was Mr. George Girling Grange, known by the boys as 'Horsey', which had something to do with his appearance.

This was during Mr. Grange's final year at the South London public school, alma mater of PG Wodehouse, Raymond Chandler, CS Forester and Ernest Shackleton amongst others. He then retired, having taught English there for 32 years. Well-respected in all quarters, he is remembered as firm but kind. 'Horsey' was born in 1896 and spent his final years by the New Forest, where he died in 1975.

Index of First Lines

More verse from imprint illyria

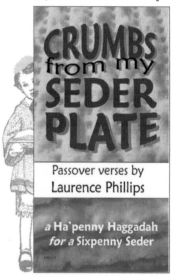